THE CHEERLEADER BOOK CLUB

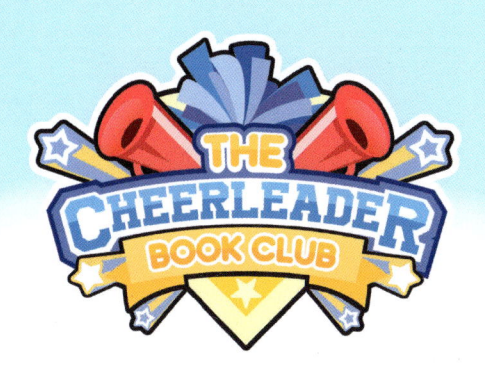

CHEER FOR YOU

WRITTEN BY ALLISON SACK

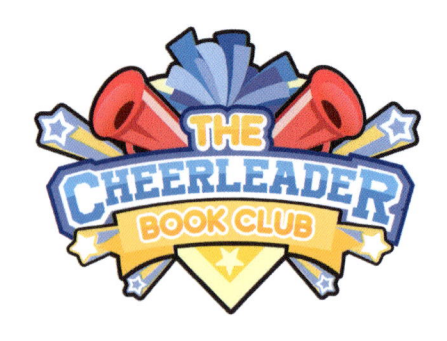

Cheer for You

© Allison Sack 2023.
All rights reserved. No parts of this book may be copied,
distributed, or published in any form without permission from the publisher,
except in the case of brief quotations embodied in reviews and certain other
noncommercial uses permitted by the copyright law.

For permissions contact through: www.thecheerleaderbookclub.com

This is a work of fiction in which all events and characters in this book are completely
imaginary. Any resemblance to actual people is entirely coincidental.

ISBN: 978-0-6486095-1-3

Written by Allison Sack
Illustrations by Nina Mkhoiani

Published by The Cheerleader Book Club

*This is for all the little ones out there
unsure about giving cheer or anything else for that matter a go.
Try it; you just might surprise yourself if you apply yourself!*

Once upon a time, in a small town, lived a little girl named Lily. She had dreams as high as the sky and a heart full of courage. Lily had always admired the cheerleaders at her school. Their stunts, their tumbles, their colourful pom-poms, and their big smiles filled her with awe.

She wanted to be just like them.

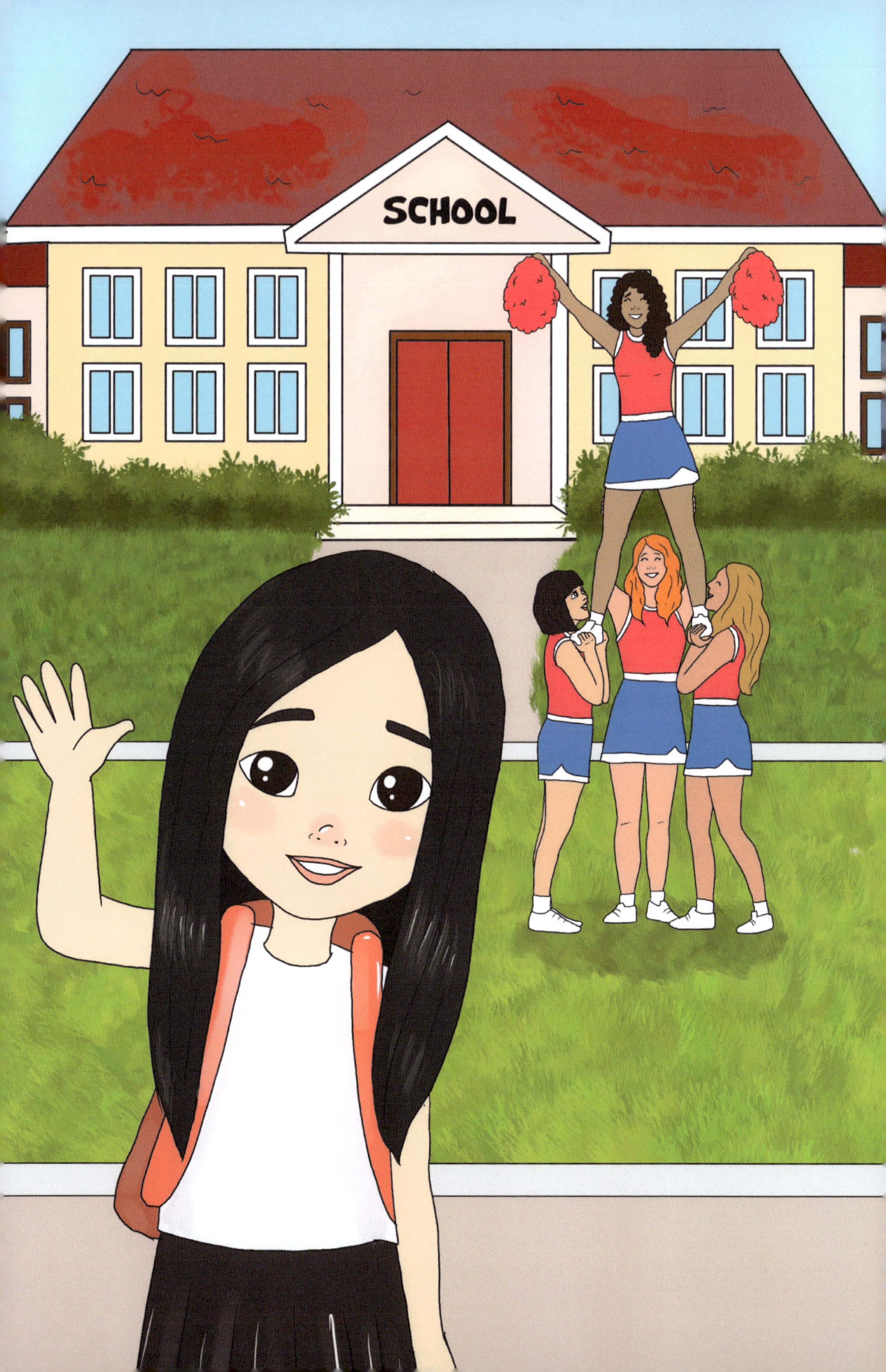
SCHOOL

One sunny morning, Lily gathered her courage and decided to attend the cheerleading tryouts at her school. But as she stood in line with other students, her heart raced, and her mind started playing tricks on her.

"I'm too tall," it was telling her.
"I can't do those splits, and I'm not strong enough."

Just then, another girl, Emily, turned to Lily and said, "Hi, I'm Emily. Is this your first time too?"

Lily smiled shyly, "Yes, I'm Lily."

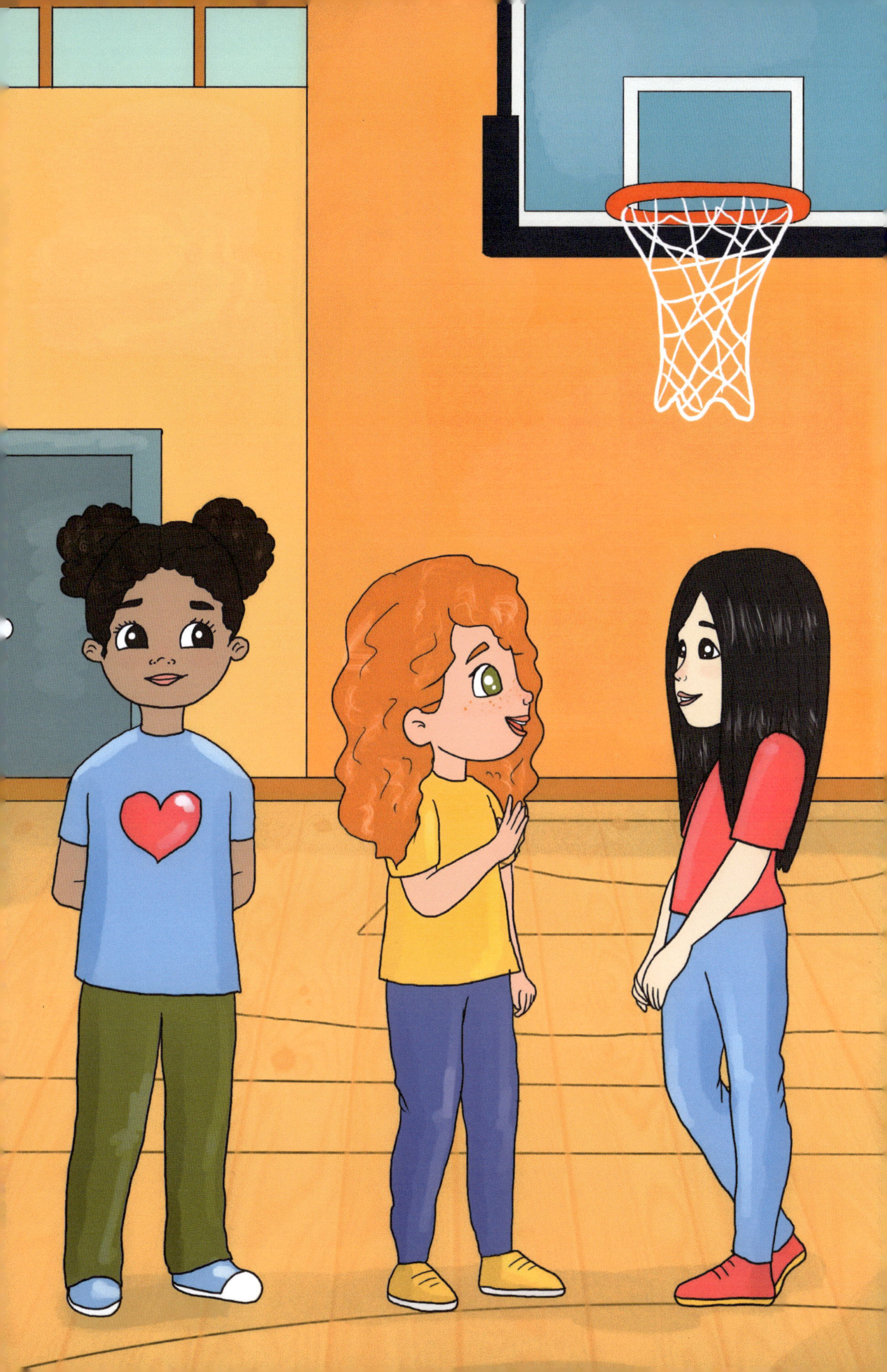

Emily was warm and friendly, and they became friends in no time. As the tryouts began, they whispered words of encouragement to each other.

Lily and Emily stepped up together when it was their turn. They tried their best to do the moves they had seen the cheerleaders do. They stumbled, giggled, and tried again.

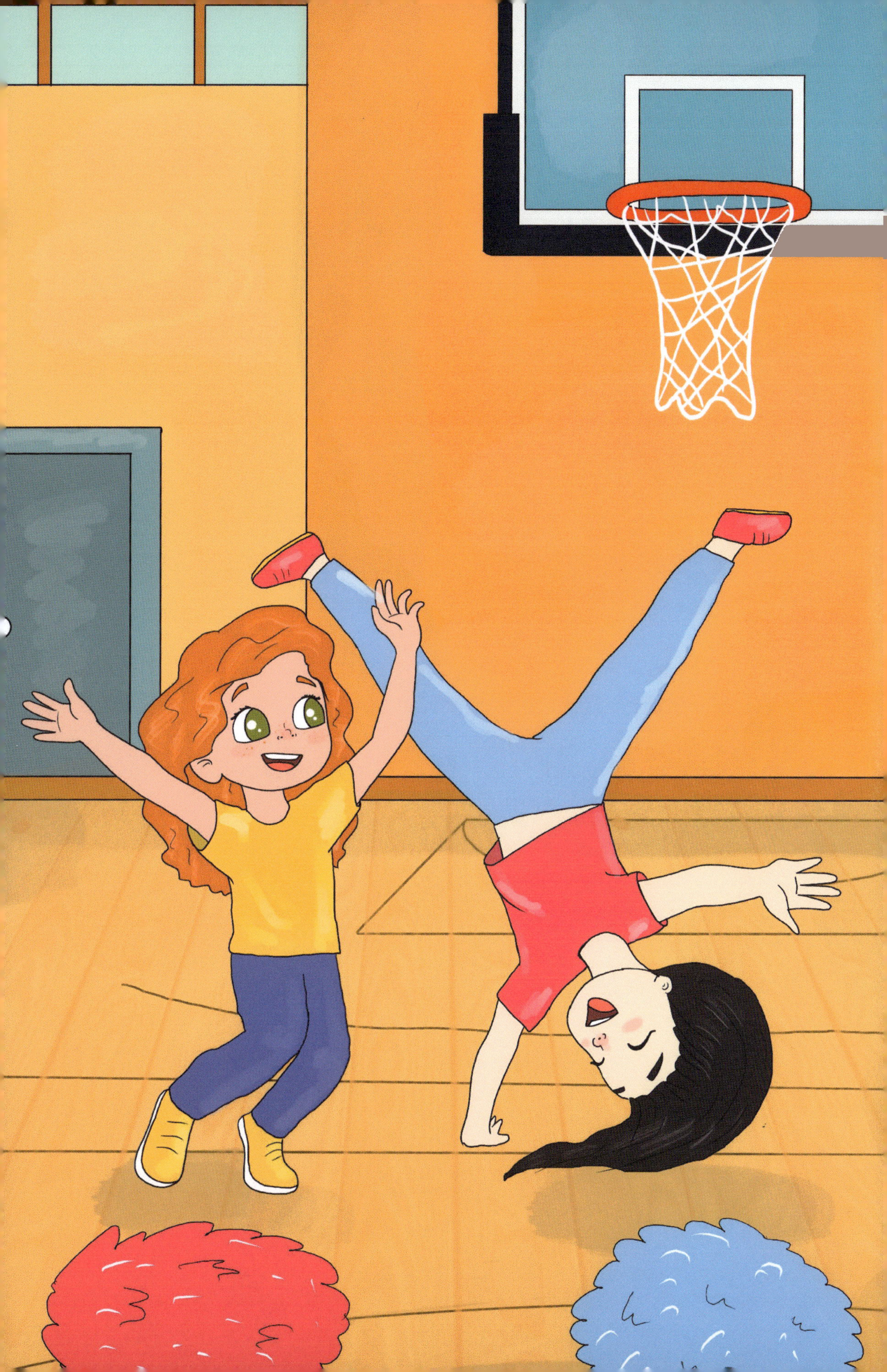

At the end of the day, Lily and Emily sat anxiously as the cheerleading coach read the names of the new team members for each team.

"Emily!" called out the coach, and Emily jumped up with joy. Lily clapped and cheered for her friend.

Then, the coach said, "Lily!" Lily couldn't believe her ears; she had made the same team as her new friend!

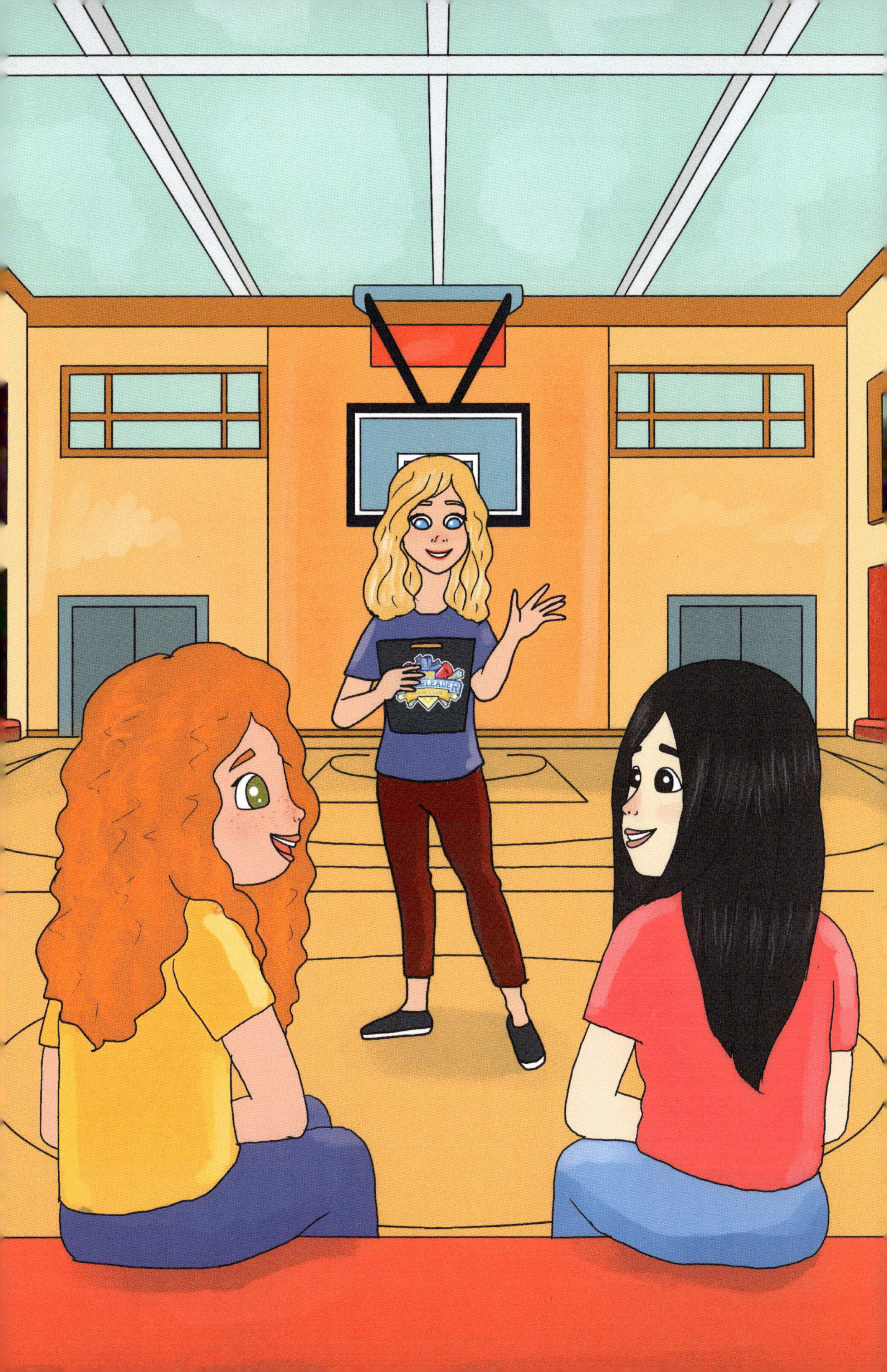

But when Lily found out her role, she wasn't so sure.

"You'll be a back spot, Lily," the coach explained.

"A back spot?" Lily asked, puzzled.

"Yes," the coach smiled. "You'll be responsible for protecting the flyer and supporting your fellow bases. You're tall and strong, Lily, and I believe you'll be great at it!"

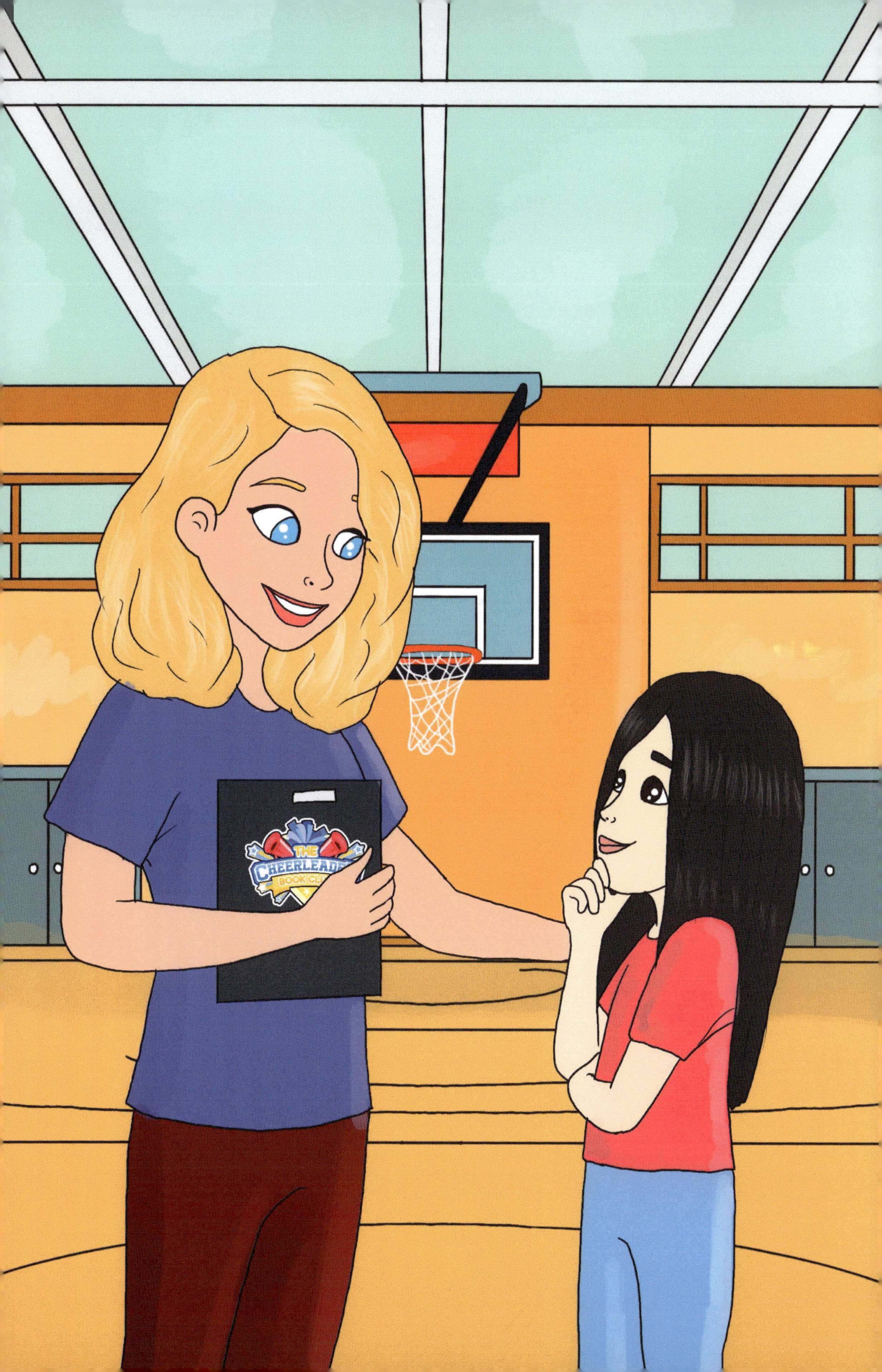
THE
CHEERLEAD
BOOK CL

Lily wasn't so sure, but with Emily's encouragement and her coach's support, she decided to give it her all.

Emily and Lily practised tirelessly. They cheered each other on, and slowly but surely, Lily began to feel more confident in her role as the back spot.

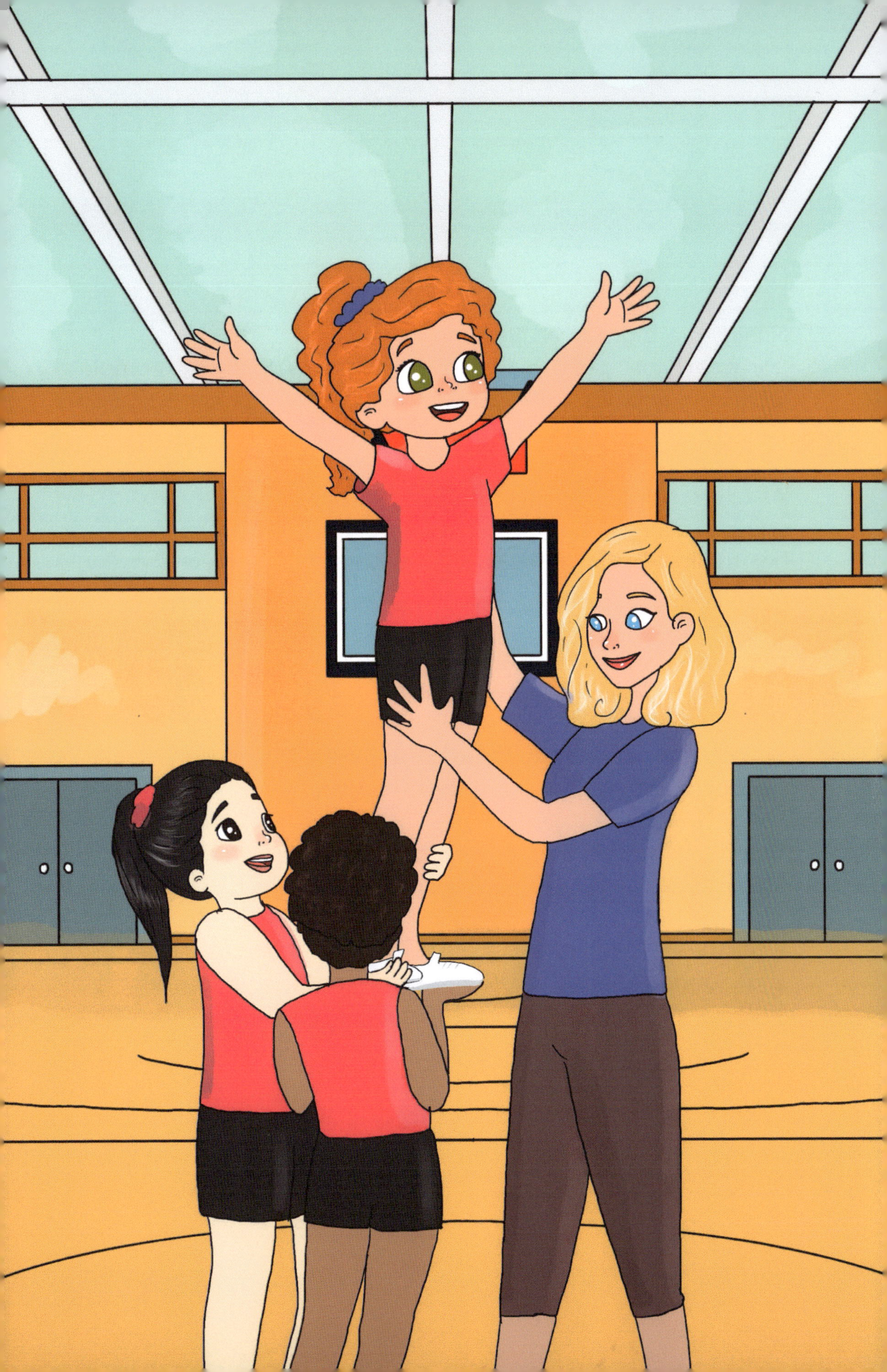

Finally, the big day arrived.
Lily and Emily put on their cheerleading uniforms, complete with sparkly bows. The stadium was filled with cheering parents and excited friends.

As Lily stood on the mat, she looked out into the crowd and saw her family waving and smiling. She could feel butterflies in her tummy, but she took a deep breath and knew she could do it.

As the music started, the butterflies disappeared, and Lily had the biggest facials. The team tumbled, cheered, and lifted their flyers high into the air, showcasing their amazing stunts and wowing the crowd. Lily focused as she performed her role as the back spot, and she did it perfectly.

The crowd erupted in cheers as the performance ended. Lily couldn't stop smiling. She had done it, and she had done it well!

After the performance, Lily and Emily shared secret handshakes and laughed together. They realised that they had not only become cheerleaders but CFF's too (Cheer Friends Forever).

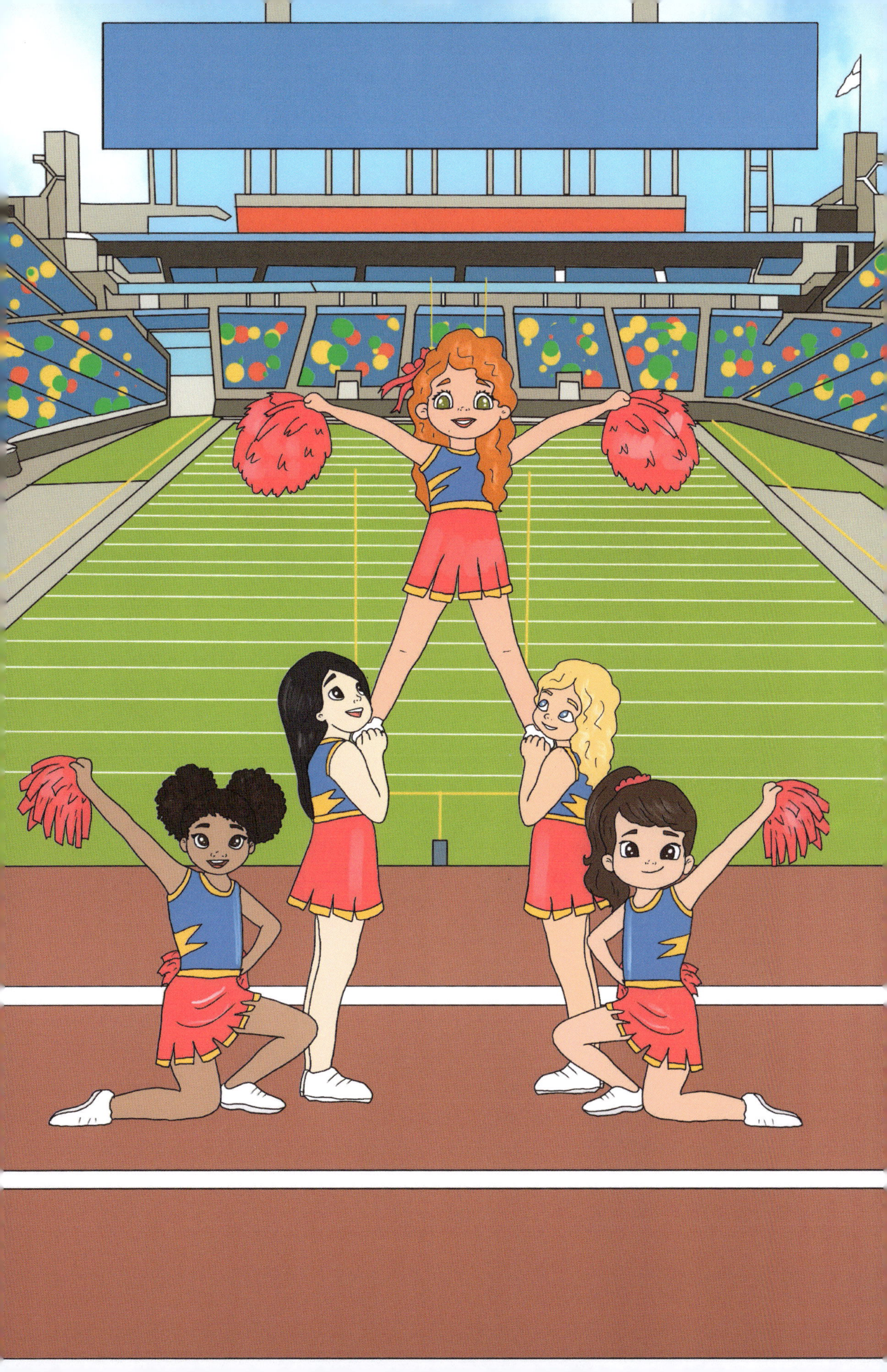

As they walked home, Lily turned to Emily and said, "You know, I was so worried about not fitting in, not being flexible enough, and not being strong enough. But I tried something new, and now it's my second family!"

Emily nodded, "And you were incredible as the back spot, Lily!"

Lily beamed with happiness. She had learned that sometimes trying something new could lead to the most wonderful surprises.

And as she looked up at the sky, she knew her dreams were closer than ever. She had cheered for herself, and it was a beautiful thing.

The end, with the biggest grin from ear to ear.

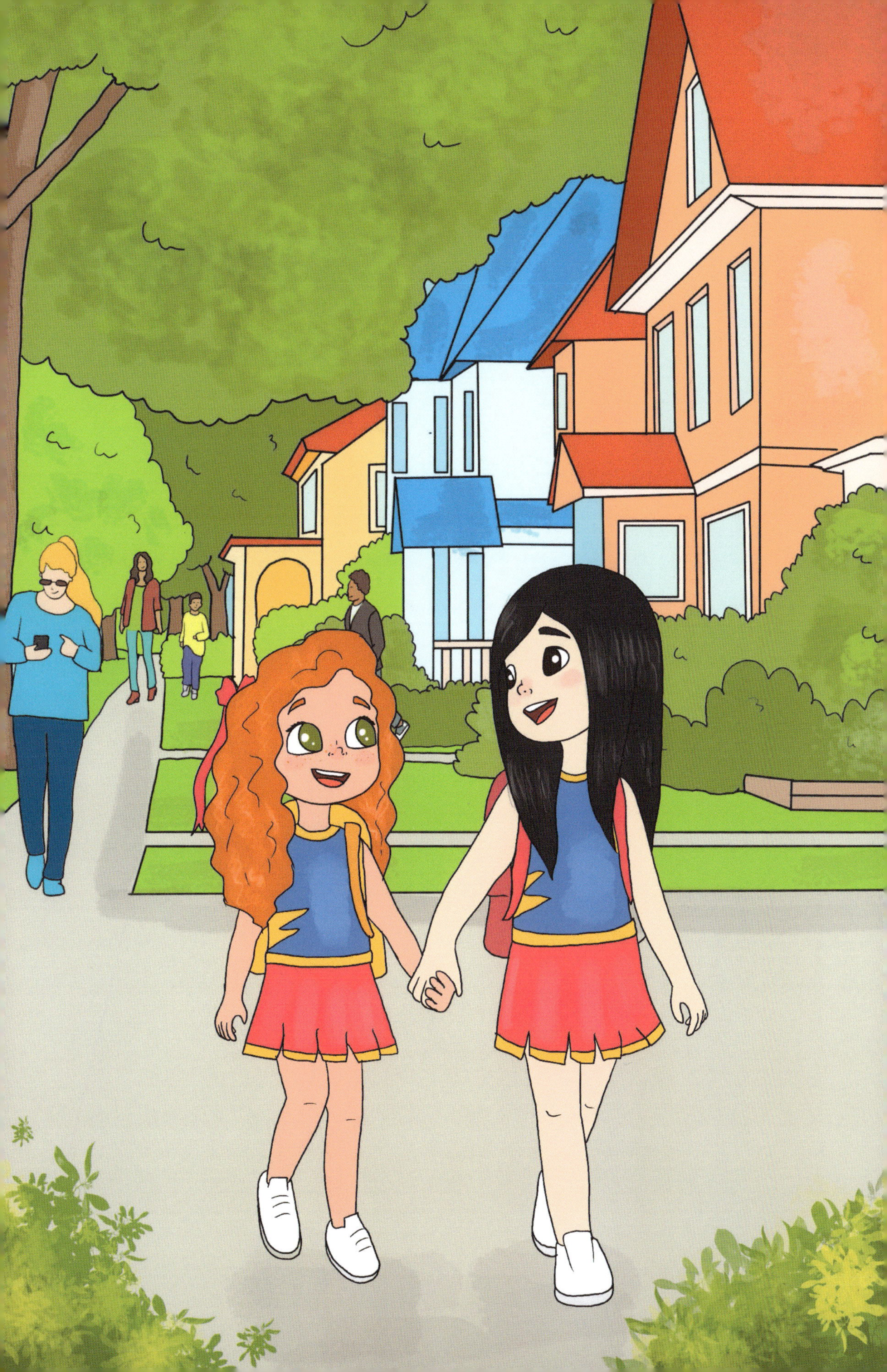

SPOT THE DIFFERENCE

There are six differences in these two pictures. Can you spot them?

FROM OUR AUTHOR:

Cheerleading has been ingrained in my spirit from day one as a coach, to an athlete, to a gym owner, to a competition event provider now, 20-something years later. Its influence changed my life to the core, touching it in profound and unimaginable ways. The opportunity to impart my passion for this sport and its positive impact on young individuals holds immeasurable value to me.

We hope your family loves these stories as much as ours.

Allison x

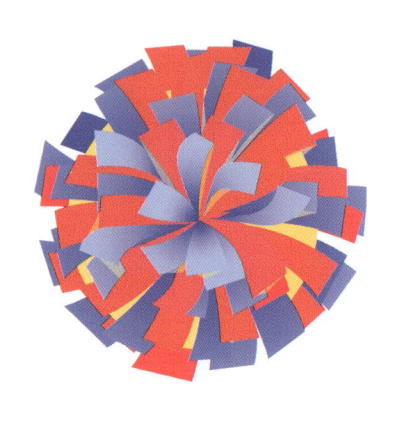

ANSWERS

THE SECRET BOOK CLUB

Head over to the website and enter the password below for access to the exclusive secret book club page!

www.thecheerleaderbookclub.com
Password: pompom2023

Here you'll be flippin' with joy for all the free downloads!

CHEERS TO YOU!

Thank you and welcome to our cheer-reading community!

Printed in Great Britain
by Amazon